YOUR PET PONY

A TRUE BOOK®

by
Elaine Landau

Children's Press®
A Division of Scholastic Inc.

New York Toronto London Auckland Sydney
Mexico City New Delhi Hong Kong
Danbury, Connecticut

Two boys riding ponies at a Los Angeles park

Content Consultant
**Robin Downing,
DVM, CVA, DAAPM**
*Hospital Director, Windsor
Veterinary Clinic
Windsor, Colorado*

Reading Consultant
Cecilia Minden-Cupp, PhD
*Former Director, Language and
Literacy Program
Harvard Graduate School of
Education*

Author's Dedication
For Ava and Julia

*The photograph on the cover
shows a young rider at the
stable. The photograph on
the title page shows an
Assateague pony.*

Library of Congress Cataloging-in-Publication Data
Landau, Elaine.
    Your pet pony / by Elaine Landau.
        p. cm. — (A true book)
    Includes index.
    ISBN-10: 0-531-16797-6 (lib. bdg.)   0-531-15463-7 (pbk.)
    ISBN-13: 978-0-531-16797-7 (lib. bdg.)   978-0-531-15463-2 (pbk.)
    1. Ponies—Juvenile literature. 2. Horsemanship—Juvenile literature. I.
Title. II. Series.
SF315.L36 2006
636.1'6–dc22

2006004422

CHILDREN'S PRESS, and A TRUE BOOK™, and associated logos are
trademarks and/or registered trademarks of Scholastic Library Publishing.
SCHOLASTIC and associated logos are trademarks and/or registered
trademarks of Scholastic Inc.
1 2 3 4 5 6 7 8 9 10 R 16 15 14 13 12 11 10 09 08 07

Contents

A rider on a Shetland pony jumps over a fence.

Pony Lovers

Do you love **ponies**? Could you see yourself galloping along the beach on a beautiful pony? Do you hope one day to ride a prize-winning pony into a show ring?

You are not alone. Many children love ponies. Some

of them and their families are thinking about buying a pony. Other children daydream about it.

Not everyone can have a pony for a pet. You need to live where you have at least 3 acres (1.2 hectares) for the pony to run. So many people keep their ponies at a stable. Keeping a pony at a stable can cost a lot of money. Caring for a pony also takes a lot of time and work.

Ponies require lots of care, including regular hoof cleaning.

Luckily, you can enjoy ponies without owning one. You can visit a local stable. You could also take lessons at a riding school or a pony club. Some summer camps have ponies. Often campers help care for them. You may just enjoy reading books and seeing movies about ponies.

So turn the page if you are a pony lover at heart. This book is all about these wonderful animals!

Visiting a local stable is one way to learn more about ponies.

Choosing the right pony can be rewarding.

Picking Out a Pony

There are many different kinds of ponies to choose from, whether you buy a pony or ride one at a stable. Is there a type, or **breed**, of pony that you like best?

Ponies come in different colors with various markings.

Colors and markings vary among these Dartmoor ponies.

There are black ponies as well as snow-white ones. Other ponies are chestnut or cream colored. Some have blonde manes and tails. Ponies can have spotted coats or patches of color.

A pony's behavior is more important than its appearance. Look for an easygoing, patient pony. You will be riding the animal, so make sure you can control it.

Pass up a handsome, highly spirited pony that might be too fast, or quick to kick or bite. You want to be safe!

A lively pony can be a challenge to ride.

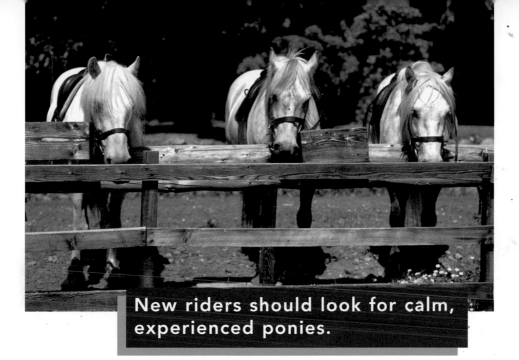

New riders should look for calm, experienced ponies.

Are you a new rider? Then you will need a particularly steady pony that won't be startled by loud noise or traffic. You want a pony that won't take off running or throw you. When a pony throws a rider, it forces the rider off its back.

These young riders may be too large for their ponies in a year.

If you and your family are looking to buy a pony, there are other things to consider. Do not pick a pony that is too small. Your pony will be fully grown when you buy it, but you are still growing. Choose a pony that you will not be too big to ride in a year or two.

Ask the seller to ride the pony for you. That way, you can see how the pony moves and behaves.

Before you buy a pony, always have a **veterinarian** look it over. The veterinarian, a doctor who treats animals, will look at the pony's teeth, eyes, legs, and hooves. A veterinarian will make sure that the pony does not have any serious conditions, such as heart disease or joint problems. The veterinarian can also help you decide if the pony is a good match for your size and ability.

A veterinarian should check the health of a horse or pony. This veterinarian examines a horse's knees.

Ponies, Ponies,

Ponies look like small horses. Yet for their size, ponies tend to be stronger than horses. Here are three of the many different breeds of ponies.

The Shetland pony is a small Scottish pony with a thick fur coat. It is about 42 inches high (107 centimeters) at the top of its shoulders. Children often ride Shetland ponies because of their size and good nature.

A Shetland pony

Ponies

A Pony of the Americas

The Pony of the Americas (POA) is perfect for the young rider who is too big for a small pony, but not ready for a full-size horse. The POA is known for its intelligence and gentle nature. It is an athletic pony that can pick up speed for games and jumps.

The Welsh pony is popular throughout the world. It is sure-footed and hardy. The Welsh pony is also an excellent jumper.

A Welsh pony and its mother

Housing a Pony

Healthy ponies need lots of time outdoors. Ponies like to **graze**, or feed on grass, stretch their legs, and run freely.

Some owners keep their ponies outside all of the time. These owners usually live on a ranch or farm or own a big

A white pony feeds on grass at the stables.

piece of land. Other owners keep their ponies at a stable.

If you and your family are thinking of keeping the pony outside, put it in a fenced-in pasture. Outdoor ponies also need a field shelter, a small barn that is open on one side. In bad weather, the pony can take cover there. A field shelter also provides shade on sunny days.

If you keep your pony in a pasture, you must check on it once or twice a day. You will want to be sure your pony

Ponies that live in pastures need visits once or twice a day.

isn't ill or injured. You also have to clean up pony droppings. Leaving them in the field isn't healthy for the pony.

Owners without land often **board**, or house, their pony at a stable. There are different ways to board ponies.

Full board means full-time housing, food, and care for a pony. Stable workers feed, **groom**, and clean up after the pony. They also exercise the pony and check its health. Full board is a good choice for busy people who do not ride their ponies very often. However, it is expensive.

Many owners board their ponies at a stable full-time.

You can also board
your pony at a stable and
take care of it yourself.
This is cheaper, but a lot
more work. Your pony will

Mucking out the stall means cleaning out the manure, or droppings.

have a small area in a stable, called a **stall**.

Because your pony lives in a small space, you must keep

the stall clean. This means cleaning it daily. Removing animal droppings, or **manure**, from a stall is known as **mucking out**.

You also have to visit the stable to feed, groom, and exercise your pony. Stabled ponies should spend part of their day outdoors. If you can't go every day, you will have to ask a friend or pay someone at the stable to help you.

Some stabled ponies develop problems living in a small space. They may bite or chew on their stall door. Or they may sway their head from side to side, a behavior known as **weaving**. Often, these ponies are better off outdoors.

If you cannot keep your pony outside, give it as much outdoor time as possible. Be sure your pony gets the exercise it needs

A stabled pony sticks its head out over the stall door to watch the yard activity.

by riding it a lot. Most young riders enjoy this as much as their ponies do!

Taking Care of Tack

A pony's bridle and bit

Tack is the gear you put on the pony for riding. A saddle is the leather seat on the pony's back. A bridle is the leather strap that fits around the pony's head and mouth. A bit is the metal part of the bridle that goes in the pony's mouth. The reins are straps fastened to the bit. The rider uses the reins to control the animal.

Carrying a pony saddle

Some people say caring for tack is almost as much work as caring for a pony! It is important to keep the pony's tack soft and clean. After each ride, wipe the mud and sweat from the leather with a damp cloth and a mild cleanser called saddle soap. Clean all the equipment thoroughly with saddle soap and water once a week.

A Pony's Food and Health

Ponies are not picky eaters. An outdoor pony eats mostly grass. When there isn't enough grass cover, you can feed your pony a special mixture of rolled oats, corn, and molasses called an oat mix.

Ponies enjoy crunching on carrots.

Stabled ponies eat mostly grain and hay. Feed your pony at the same times each day. Like most animals, ponies enjoy routine. They like carrots, apples, and turnips, too.

Feed your pony a few small meals instead of one large meal. It is easier for your pony to digest smaller amounts.

A pony nibbles on fresh hay outside a stable.

All ponies need fresh, clean water.

Your pony needs regular visits with a veterinarian. A veterinarian gives ponies shots to prevent disease.

A veterinarian will also check the pony's teeth. Teeth can grow sharp from uneven wear, making it difficult for the animal to eat properly. The veterinarian corrects the problem by filing down the teeth.

You must be aware of your pony's mood and health.

You must be alert to your pony's needs. Don't ignore important signs. If your pony is sweating, has difficulty breathing, or shows little energy, it may be ill. Swollen legs or dripping from the nose or eyes can mean illness as well.

Tell your concerns immediately to the adult who is helping you care for your pony. When your pony is sick or injured, call a veterinarian.

You and Your Pony

Whether you own a pony or ride one at a stable, you will enjoy spending time with your pony. You may ride it on trails just for fun, or you may practice jumps with your pony.

In time, you may decide to enter a riding or jumping

A young rider practices on a course.

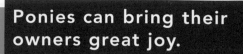
Ponies can bring their owners great joy.

competition. Winning at a horse or pony show can be an exciting experience.

However, caring for a pony is a big responsibility. The animal will depend on you to feed, care, groom, and exercise it. It is also up to you to be sure the pony gets the help it needs if it becomes injured or ill. Having a happy, healthy pony to love and care for is the best prize of all.

To Find Out More

Here are some additional resources to help you learn more about ponies:

 **Books**

Barnes, Julia. **101 Facts About Horses and Ponies**. Gareth Stevens, 2002.

Gaff, Jackie. **I Wonder Why Horses Wear Shoes and Other Questions About Horses**. Kingfisher, 2002.

Henderson, Carolyn. **Pony Care: A Young Rider's Guide**. DK Publishing, 2005.

Holub, Joan. **Why Do Horses Neigh?** Dial Books for Young Readers, 2003.

Kalman, Bobbie. **Ponies**. Crabtree Publishing, 2004.

Ransford, Sandy. **The Kingfisher Illustrated Horse and Pony Encyclopedia**. Kingfisher, 2004.

Staff of Pleasant Company Publications. **Girls and Their Horses: True Tales from American Girls**. Pleasant Company Publications, 2000.

Organizations and Online Sites

American Shetland Pony Club
81 B Queenwood Road
Morton, IL 61550
309–263–4044
http://www.shetlandminiature.com

Visit this site to learn more about the latest Shetland news and events. Be sure to check out the "Kids' Room" link.

American Society for the Prevention of Cruelty to Animals (ASPCA)
424 East 92nd Street
New York, NY 10128
212–876–7700
http://www.aspca.org

This organization's site has extensive information on horse care, including tips on training, handling, and nutritional needs.

American Youth Horse Council
http://www.ayhc.com

Check out this nonprofit organization's site to read its newsletter and useful brochures.

Pony of the Americas Club, Inc.
5240 Elmwood Avenue
Indianapolis, IN 46203
317–788–0107
http://www.poac.org

This international organization is dedicated to the POA breed and young riders. Its site offers a photo gallery, an online magazine, and details about upcoming show events.

United States Pony Clubs, Inc.
4041 Iron Works Parkway
Lexington, KY 40511
859–254–7669
http://www.ponyclub.org

With local branches all over the world, this club provides junior riders with opportunities for instruction and competition. Look at this site for information about horse-related activities in your area.

Important Words

board to house

breed a specific type of animal

full board full-time housing, food, and care for a horse or pony

graze to feed on grass

groom to clean an animal

manure animal droppings

mucking out removing manure from a stall

ponies small horses, especially horse breeds that stay small as adults

stall a small area in a stable that houses a pony or horse

veterinarian a doctor who treats animals

weaving a problem behavior, often seen in stabled ponies, of swaying the head from side to side

Index

Meet the Author

Award-winning author Elaine Landau worked as a newspaper reporter, an editor, and a youth-services librarian before becoming a full-time writer. She has written more than 250 nonfiction books for young people, including True Books on dinosaurs, animals, countries, and food. Ms. Landau has a bachelor's degree in English and journalism from New York University as well as a master's degree in library and information science. She lives with her husband and son in Miami, Florida.